E242
EDUCATION: A SECOND-LEVEL COURSE

LEARNING FOR ALL

UNIT 16

LEARNING FOR ALL

Prepared for the course team by
Felicity Armstrong and Tony Booth

The Open University

E242 COURSE READERS

There are two course readers associated with E242; they are:
BOOTH, T., SWANN, W., MASTERTON, M. and POTTS, P. (eds) (1992) *Learning for All 1: curricula for diversity in education*, London, Routledge/The Open University (**Reader 1**).

BOOTH, T., SWANN, W., MASTERTON, M. and POTTS, P. (eds) (1992) *Learning for All 2: policies for diversity in education*, London, Routledge/The Open University (**Reader 2**).

TELEVISION PROGRAMMES AND AUDIO-CASSETTES

There are eight TV programmes and two audio-cassettes associated with E242. They are closely integrated into the unit texts and there are no separate TV or cassette notes. However, further information about them may be obtained by writing to Open University Educational Enterprises Ltd, 12 Cofferidge Close, Stony Stratford, Milton Keynes MK11 1BY.

Cover illustration shows a detail from *Midsummer Common* by Dorothy Bordass.

The Open University, Walton Hall, Milton Keynes MK7 6AA

First published 1992. This edition published 1996.

Edited, designed and typeset by The Open University.

Printed in the United Kingdom by Page Bros, Norwich

ISBN 0 7492 7577 4

This unit forms part of an Open University course; the complete list of units is printed at the end of this book. If you have not enrolled on the course and would like to buy this or other Open University material, please write to Open University Educational Enterprises Ltd, 12 Cofferidge Close, Stony Stratford MK11 1BY, United Kingdom. If you wish to enquire about enrolling as an Open University student, please write to the Admissions Office, The Open University, PO Box 48, Walton Hall, Milton Keynes MK7 6AB, United Kingdom.

2.1

13630C/e242u16i2.1

CONTENTS

1 INTRODUCTION

1.1 In this final unit we will provide you with opportunities to reflect on concerns raised by the course. In Unit 14/15, you explored the sources of power in the system. In concentrating on official sources of power we may have unwittingly enhanced their value by contributing to the sense of powerlessness to influence education felt by many teachers, parents and school students. However, official policies, including legislation, represent only one set of influences affecting education and their effect depends on the way they are treated by practitioners. It is one of the aims of this course to extend *your* influence on education by encouraging you to link ideas about practice to a firm set of principles. The more *you* influence education, the less it will depend on other forces.

1.2 The three main sections of this unit serve different purposes and you should be prepared for shifts of focus as you move from one to the other. Section 2 of this unit, 'Responding to difference at Hirst High', is a case study of the way one comprehensive school divided and categorized its students according to their attainment and assumptions about their ability. We examined the school at the point when it had just included a group of students categorized as having 'severe learning difficulties'. To what extent can a comprehensive school provide a learning environment in which all students participate and are positively valued irrespective of their level of attainment or disability? How do the new students fit into the pre-existing culture and structure of the school? Our case study provides an opportunity to reflect on the effects of grouping and setting policies. It is also a reminder of the complexity of schools and the need to avoid generalizations about the way they operate.

1.3 In Section 3, 'Controlling change', we discuss the information about difficulties in learning that schools are required to present to parents and examine the scope for those working in mainstream and special schools and colleges to take control of their own policies. We consider the possibilities for formal school development plans to enable staff in schools to absorb official pressures into their own values and approaches to education. We will consider the perspective of those working within special schools and look at two examples of special schools that have deliberately changed their roles.

1.4 The final section of the unit, 'A common concern', asks you to reflect on the principles underlying the course and their practical implications. Unless you stumbled into the course by accident you will share with other course participants, and with ourselves, concerns for students who experience difficulties in education and for disabled students. Students may experience difficulties either in interpreting the curriculum or may bring their vulnerabilities to school or be made vulnerable once they are there. In what ways do our concerns limit the range of principles and practices that we should adopt in education?

1.5   This unit should take up two weeks study time. Section 2 is the longest part of the unit but Section 3, which includes three chapters from Reader 2, involves more reading overall. Listed below is the material other than this text that you will study in each section, and where it can be found.

Section 2 Responding to difference at Hirst High

Cassette 2, Programme 4: *Responding to Difference.*

Section 3 Controlling change

Reader 2, Chapter 3: 'Planning school development' by Christine Gilbert.

Reader 2, Chapter 4: 'Finding a new place: changes in role at Ormerod Special School' by Tim Southgate.

Reader 2, Chapter 5: 'Moving in and moving out: the closure of Etton Pasture Special School' by Roger Kidd.

Section 4 A common concern

No additional material.

2   RESPONDING TO DIFFERENCE AT HIRST HIGH

2.1   In this section we provide a detailed description of the way a comprehensive school has responded to the diversity of its students with a particular focus on differences of attainment. We look at the consequence that this has for the relationships between students and their opportunities for learning.

2.2   We chose the school because of its strong relationship with the communities it serves and because the school had recently included a group of students categorized as having 'severe learning difficulties', drawn from across the south of Northumberland. We were interested to see how this new group of students would be accommodated within the existing school structures and whether their presence in the school would affect the approach to education for all students.

2.3   Although the new group of students were all assigned to the same 'special needs' category, they had a broad range of interests and attainments. However, they included some students who had shown little evidence of understanding of language or capacity for voluntary movement. Such students are sometimes thought to be among the most difficult to include within the mainstream, particularly after primary age. If they can participate in a comprehensive secondary education, what reason is there for excluding other students who may experience less severe difficulties?

2.4   The model of inclusion at Hirst High, based on the groupings of the special school system it replaced, is only one possible way of including such students. Kenn Jupp, the head of Overdale Special School in Stockport for primary-aged students categorized as having severe learning difficulties, established a pilot scheme whereby five students chosen randomly from his school attended their local primary school. Each child was supported by a full-time learning support assistant. A peripatetic specialist teacher provided teaching support to all five schools. Despite the apparent success of the project, when the local authority planned to extend the project, it opted (to the disappointment of Kenn Jupp) for a system of resourced schools where five or six students from Overdale would be grouped in one school. These children, however, would be supported within mainstream classes (Jupp, 1992).

2.5   This section describes Hirst High in the early stages of the inclusion of the new group of students. We start by examining, briefly, the ethos and structure of the high school since it opened, the background to the closure of Riverbank Special School and the approach to integration. We then introduce the cassette programme which concentrates on the first half of our story of the school, the way the school divided students by attainment and presumed ability and structured its time before it was joined by students from Riverbank Special School. We then take up the story of the inclusion of the new group of students and staff at the school.

BACKGROUND TO A DEVELOPING SCHOOL

2.6   Hirst High School is a mixed comprehensive school, built in 1974, with about 800 students aged 13 to 18 years (year 9 onwards). It is on the edge of a large housing estate in Ashington, north of Newcastle. It was formed from an amalgamation of two secondary modern schools which had become co-educational a year earlier. This was once a thriving mining and fishing community but both industries have virtually collapsed in the area. ALCAN, the aluminium smelter, was the main provider of employment but has laid off large numbers of workers. Unemployment, particularly for men, is endemic in the area.

2.7   Richard Houlden was appointed as the head teacher when the school opened and has remained since. He explained how the school set out to sever its culture from that in the secondary modern schools from which it had emerged. The staff wanted the school to be 'achievement oriented' and this is reflected in the 'hall of fame' in the entrance area to

Pit ponies with Ashington Colliery in the background. Untitled painting by Oliver Kilbourne of the Ashington Group (1959), courtesy Woodhorn Colliery Museum/Ashington Group Trustees.

Ashington was once a thriving mining community, but most of the pits in the area have now closed down.

Woodhorn Colliery closed in 1981 and is now a museum.

the school, where there are photographs and descriptions of students who have gone on to university. The staff devised a system of mixed attainment tutor groups from which students were assigned to multiple sets for a variety of subjects based on their attainments. The setting system of the first-year students (year 9) gave way to option choices in the 14+ curriculum, where the school adopted a broad concept of achievement, and there was strong encouragement to students to stay on in the sixth form.

2.8   The way the learning difficulties of students were identified and supported underwent a series of changes which were similar to those described in Units 1/2 and 6/7. Gwen Woodman, the co-ordinator for learning support and a member of the senior management team in the school, described developments in learning support from the mid-eighties:

> ... about five or six years ago these special needs students in mainstream were part of what you would call the remedial provision where most of their time was spent with one or two teachers, very limited curriculum, very limited access to facilities. About five years ago we embarked upon a very large programme of staff in-service. Out of this came a change in provision so that all of the youngsters had total access to the curriculum and to all areas of the school and consequently access to all staff.

2.9   In practice, this meant that instead of being in a remedial class taught by a single teacher, the students with the lowest attainments became the lowest set. Any teacher might be timetabled to teach them. Initially students identified as having 'special needs' were offered in-class support, but Gwen Woodman argued that the setting system and the increase in contact and confidence between teachers and these students enabled this to be reduced. She provides additional English for this bottom set during four out of the six French lessons in a ten-day cycle.

2.10   The buildings and facilities are available to local people for educational and leisure activities. They share the library and are welcome to join students and staff for lunch. The cuts to the local authority budget in the early 1990s had put a large number of community education projects at risk and pushed class sizes up and reduced planning time for teachers.

The closure of Riverbank Special School

2.11   In the early 1980s, Riverbank was an 'all-age' school for students described as having 'severe or profound learning difficulties', split between two sites, one for primary and the other for secondary students. The buildings needed improvement and were overcrowded. The county council had planned to rebuild the school on a greenfield site when funds 'became available'. However, because of pressure on space during 1984–5 children of first-school age moved to spare accommodation on the same site as Abbeyfield First School in Morpeth.

2.12   An initial wariness from both sets of parents changed to a view that there were advantages for all children and the children shared an increasing number of activities. Building adaptations were made and the new students transferred to the school roll. The successful experience at Abbeyfield was a major factor in the decision to make similar amalgamations with Hirst High and the adjacent middle school. Major changes were made to both schools, with purpose-built suites including rooms for speech therapy and physiotherapy and, at the middle school, a hydrotherapy pool.

GROUPS AND TIMETABLES: CONSTRAINTS ON PARTICIPATION

2.13   The arrival of the Riverbank students at Hirst High created a categorization problem. Within the school a group of students, placed in a bottom set on entry to the school, were already spoken of as having 'special needs' and the teacher with responsibility for them, Gwen Woodman, was the 'co-ordinator for special needs'. The students and staff from Riverbank were based in a new 'department of special needs' in Hirst High and their head of department, Eileen Farnham, who had previously been head of the senior Riverbank department, was described as the head of the special needs department. Gwen Woodman was given responsibility for ensuring smooth communication between school management and the new department and she subsequently relabelled her activities as 'learning support'. As you attempt to understand our description of the school you have to be aware of the ways in which the term 'special needs' was used in the school and the roles of various members of staff.

Activity 1   Responding to difference

Cassette 2, Programme 4, is called *Responding to Difference*. It introduces you to some of the teachers and students at Hirst High. They describe the way students are categorized by attainment within the school and the consequences this has for the gender composition of groups. They discuss the school timetable and the reasons for it. The programme asks how the students who had recently arrived from Riverbank Special School might participate in the school.

The programme opens with an extract from a GCSE lesson in which students were asked to prepare a short improvization on the situations in which it would be appropriate to use standard English and those where it would be appropriate to use the dialect of the North East. We used this sequence to provoke thought about the subtle ways in which students may be categorized in schools and the value that may attach to them as a result.

Listen to Cassette 2, Programme 4, now.

As you listen to the programme, think about the following questions:

* What effects do the grouping policies have on the way students learn and the difficulties they encounter?

* In particular, what effects do the grouping policies have on the way school achievement is perceived by boys and girls?

* What effects do pre-existing grouping policies have for the inclusion of students categorized as having 'severe learning difficulties' within the school?

2.14   In responding to the cassette programme, we have concentrated on the second half of the story about the inclusion of students from Riverbank school, which is only barely introduced in the programme. However, we have also added a number of comments on the grouping and timetabling arrangements for the whole school and reinforced others. The opening sequence to the programme, a mock interview with the Newcastle United manager, was recorded when the team were close to the bottom of the second division of the football league. In early 1996, Newcastle may win the premier league. Such a change in fortunes would have affected the way the manager was portrayed. The lesson illustrated the way that different dialects might be 'appropriate' for different audiences but it was clear that it raised questions about the accents and forms of expression that would be valued within schools and the effects this might have on students' readiness and capacities for learning.

2.15   Hirst High School provides a contrast to Whitmore High School's mixed-attainment grouping policy, which is described in Unit 1/2 (pp. 71–9) and later in this unit in the reading on development plans (Reader 2, Chapter 3). It is the system at Whitmore school which is the more unusual. Dividing students into different groupings according to attainment and perceived ability is commonplace at secondary schools. The way it is done varies between schools and within subject areas, but there are very few schools where there is no streaming or setting of any kind. In Northumberland, according to one local authority officer, students are set in some way at all high schools, and some middle schools adopt a system of setting from the age of nine. At Hirst High the head linked the policy of setting to a desire for the school to be, and to be seen as, achievement oriented. The majority of pupils in the school (but not those who were part of the special needs department) belonged to mixed-attainment tutor groups and spent the last period each day with their tutor. But setting was routine across the curriculum.

2.16   In the programme, four main reasons were given for setting:

- It is easier to give pupils the kinds of courses they need; these different courses are designed to respond to differences in perceived ability.
- Mixed-attainment teaching 'holds the brighter ones back'.
- It is easier to teach groups of pupils who are divided up according to attainment.
- Setting makes it possible to meet the needs of all pupils.

2.17   Although, in theory, students could have been in different sets for different subjects, most departments followed the setting decisions made by the maths and English departments. The French department, for example, allocated students to its sets on the basis of the sets they were in for English. The science department had a rather different system, there was a set 1 and a set 2 with the rest of the students divided randomly between three further sets, said to be 'mixed-ability'. But in what sense were these 'mixed ability' if the pupils seen as the highest attainers in science were extracted? However, such an arrangement did avoid the stigma and gender segregation and behaviour difficulties associated with a fifth set.

Setting for 'learning support'

2.18   Students were allocated to sets when they arrived at the school in year 9. Gwen Woodman, the co-ordinator for 'learning support', identified students who needed 'learning support' while they were at their middle schools and placed them in set 5 for English. Since modern language sets are based on English sets, she could withdraw them from modern languages for four of their lessons and give them help with their English to 'get their skills boosted up … in the year 9'. There were a number of implications of this policy. It was even harder for these students than others to move to a higher set once they had arrived at the school with a 'special needs' label. Withdrawal from French on a regular basis limited their future option choices.

2.19   Besides withdrawing students in year 9 for additional English, Gwen Woodman taught the lower-attaining option groups in year 10 and 11 for English lessons.

Sets for units of accreditation

2.20   For years 10 and 11, students were divided, for any particular subject, between GCSE and units of accreditation groups. The latter course consisted of short modules which were individually assessed and recorded on a certificate. An English teacher explained the advantages of the system of units of accreditation compared to what was on offer at her previous school:

> There was nothing like that so the ones at the bottom ended up with nothing. The most important thing is that the ones in the bottom set have something to work for, so when they leave some of them have piles of certificates saying exactly what they have done. One of the problems with those groups is truancy, so if you've got some who don't come to school regularly they can much more easily pick it up when they come back and it doesn't matter if they are not doing the same as everybody else.

Setting by gender

2.21   The most striking unplanned consequence of the setting system was the overwhelming predominance of girls in 'top' sets and boys in 'bottom' sets. Only in set 3 did there appear to be fairly equal numbers. This led, too, to an imbalance of the sexes in PE and games groups, because these were timetabled against languages.

2.22   The school staff were well aware of the unequal achievement of girls and boys, the fact that boys were less positive about school than girls and of the need to do something about both of these issues. Some teachers suggested that boys were in lower sets as this was a consequence of setting by ability. Other teachers and some students suggested that boys were in lower sets because of their behaviour. Disruptive behaviour can itself be an expression of negative attitudes to what is being offered in school or an expression of hopelessness about prospects in an area of high unemployment. It could be that the setting system reinforced or produced, in part, differences in attainment and

One by-product of the setting system was the overwhelming preponderance of girls in top sets …

… and boys in lower sets.

12

behaviour between groups. Could adjustments to the setting system be part of a strategy to raise the achievement of boys without interfering in the learning of girls?

Staff sets

2.23   At Hirst High, the head teacher and the three deputy heads were men. In common with a majority of secondary schools and most other institutions there are few women in senior management positions. One could argue that in the adult community there is a predominance of males in the 'top set'. How do students and staff make sense of this?

Students' views of setting

2.24   We asked neither staff nor students about their views of staff sets, but we did ask students what they felt about student sets. The answers we obtained contradicted any presumption that students in lower sets would uniformly object to the system and their place within it. At Hirst High teachers went to considerable lengths to positively value the learning of students and we gained the impression that most students recognized this whatever set they were in. Of course, most had gone through middle schools where setting was accepted, particularly in the upper years, so they may not have had recent experience of mixed-attainment teaching groups to compare with their current situation.

2.25   There was general agreement that it was possible to move between sets which was clearly a motivating factor for some pupils. However, students also expressed doubts about whether teachers would detect that a student was in the 'wrong' set.

2.26   Several students did feel that the setting system led to the positive and negative labelling of pupils as 'brainy' or 'thick', and that students felt unhappy about themselves if they were moved from an upper to a lower set. They argued too, that students from top and bottom sets did not mix much socially which may have had particular effects on relationships between boys and girls at this school given the gender imbalances in sets.

2.27   On the cassette programme, Michael described a system in which pupils would not be divided up into different sets but would help each other learn in groups:

> If you haven't got top sets and bottom sets, like, the not so brainy ones will learn off you and you'll learn more off the teacher so it's in a chain … If one says 'Oh, what's …?' and the brainy one says, 'Oh such and such …' And it could be his friend who's not so brainy and he says, 'Why, the teacher didn't tell us that but *you* told us so we're one step forward!'

The timetable: from six days to ten

2.28 In the programme, Bill Gould explained the particular local characteristics which he felt were important in deciding on the timetable. He had felt that only by having a six-day timetable could the school mitigate the problem of certain lessons being regularly missed by some pupils because of working patterns in the mines and market day.

2.29 There were a number of reasons given for changing from a six-day to a ten-day timetable. The 60 slots available over a ten-day cycle made it easier for the timetabler to respond to the intricate demands of the national curriculum. The six-day timetable made it difficult to organize activities with agencies outside the school, such as regular joint sporting activities with other schools. It had posed particular difficulties in relation to visits from Riverbank school before its students transferred to Hirst High. One teacher argued that the school should go one step further and make the timetable conform to the real world of days of the week.

Activity 2　In the interests of the timetable

How do you respond to the arguments for a 60-period ten-day timetable? How far can a secondary timetable be simplified? How does it constrain the organization of the curriculum and the participation of students?

2.30 The arguments presented for the 60-period ten-day timetable are only partly concerned with the effective learning of students. Many teachers argue that students learn best with the minimum changes of teachers and subject matter. If this is so, then it is illogical to argue that the teaching of the national curriculum requires greater fragmentation of student experience, for the effective teaching of the national curriculum, as of other curricula, must depend on the creation of good conditions for learning. If it is not realistic to build a timetable around the learning needs of students, what are schools for?

FROM RIVERBANK SCHOOL TO THE SPECIAL NEEDS DEPARTMENT

2.31 In October 1991, 29 students, six teachers, six teaching assistants, a full-time physiotherapist, and a speech therapist visiting one day a week became the new special needs department at Hirst High. This notion that the students and staff constituted a 'department', like other departments at the school such as maths or modern languages, may have made it seem natural, to many, that the students should spend most of their time there: maths teachers teach maths students and 'special needs' teachers teach 'special needs' students. Yet the special needs department, unlike any other department of the school, was expected to deliver the bulk of the curriculum to its students.

2.32   The confusion of terms between mainstream and 'special needs' was eased by making one of Gwen Woodman's roles that of 'co-ordinator of learning support'. But there was another consequence of moving Riverbank students into a 'special needs' department. Although they had joined a mainstream school, most staff referred to them as 'special needs students', differentiated from the rest of the students who were 'mainstream' students.

2.33   Before they joined the school, the staff at Riverbank had been moving away from attainment grouping, according to a pattern familiar to you from reading Jenny Corbett's study for Unit 8/9 (Reader 2, Chapter 17). They had taught a 'special care' group in isolation from others, but decided to group students by age in mixed attainment groups, each with a teacher and teaching assistant.

2.34   It was as if the division between special care and other students was being recreated within Hirst High, but now all the ex-Riverbank students were being assigned to the special category. The experience was rather like that at Springfield Road Junior School before the staff decided to amalgamate the severe learning difficulties unit with the rest of the school (Booth and Jones, 1987). When students from the unit there visited mainstream classes, they were known as 'special needs' or even 'units'. Once they were on the class register of mainstream classes, they were referred to by their names.

2.35   It seemed that the divisions might be broken down if the students from Riverbank could become members of the mixed-attainment tutor groups and this was supported by some teachers and a majority of the students to whom we spoke. However, this required a far greater change in thinking within the school than we had imagined. If it were to happen it would take place only after gradually increasing contact of staff and students.

2.36   Eileen Farnham had expected that the school would develop a clear plan for increasing the participation of Riverbank students, which would then be implemented and supported. Instead she had to work with a more gradual policy involving increasing contact with staff and students but with no explicit agenda. The head teacher expressed the ambivalence of some staff towards accommodating the new students:

> You have to move towards integration slowly. I don't think you can rush it. Attitudes have to change and develop. People need to have time to come to terms with it. Certainly in terms of the philosophy of the special needs department we believed they needed a secure base and they can get themselves established there and then they can move out. But perhaps in concentrating on *them* needing a secure base, we also recognize that *we* needed them to have a secure base ...

2.37   For some, the initial contacts emphasized differences in culture between the groups. Students and staff were on first-name terms in Riverbank, there was no uniform and there were fewer rules. One teacher described how she responded to being part of a larger, more complex and rule-governed organization after knowing the small, more relaxed community at Riverbank:

> They have obviously got to have rules which we didn't have to have in a smaller school. We had this small organization, this smaller sort of society where we didn't have to have so many rules. Now we've got to sort of 'police' our end of the corridor and do a break duty and I found it really difficult to say, 'What are you doing here? Should you be here? All right, but I'll have to check with your tutor.' I don't like doing it because I can't actually answer to myself why they should be outside and why they shouldn't lean on the radiator because it's lovely and warm and freezing outside. I know we're going to have to change, there's no doubt about it! Perhaps they'll have to change a little bit as well.

2.38   And there were other changes in structure to which staff had to adapt. The special needs department had been part of a special school with its own identity and hierarchy. For Eileen Farnham, the head of the new department, this involved less adaptation than, for example, the head of the middle-school department, who had been acting head of the special school. However, two members of the secondary department left, soon after the amalgamation, to work in special schools.

2.39   Riverbank staff had been used to a close relationship with the local authority who had been their employers. The rest of the school, used to devolved management, felt almost totally autonomous. The local management of special schools, promoted within the 1993 Education Act, has brought sets of staff closer together in this respect.

2.40   Hirst High offered the students a wider range of activities than those available at Riverbank. How were the students to be given access to these? They were not going to be integrated directly into the existing structures of tutor groups and sets. But the tutor groups and setting system and the 60-period, ten-day timetable were fixed points around which any participation had to be organized.

2.41   Meetings were held regularly when the team in the special needs department sat down together and considered each child individually to make sure that 'their needs were being met' and that there was a balance in the timetable. Team members were keen to benefit from the other school facilities and staff but Eileen Farnham suggested that they needed to look very closely at the content and teaching strategies of mixed lessons. While opportunities for sharing lessons and staff were welcomed, some staff worried that their careful planning of the curriculum might be upset. As one teacher put it, 'We are in danger of building our timetables around the periods which we have been offered.'

2.42   The collaboration between staff in the department and specialist subject staff was leading to greater specialization in the department. Hazel Coombs, for example, had arrived at the school after the move, and was taking responsibility for science teaching. This meant that she took groups into the science area as well as working on a science curriculum with all those within the department that the staff felt could participate. She was keen to make these real learning experiences rather than 'looking at creepy crawlies under stones again'. When we met she was working on a module on the water cycle.

Physical access

2.43   The design and layout of any institution affects the degree to which those using it can circulate freely and this in turn affects the kinds of social relationships which can develop within it. Extensive modifications were made to the buildings to make access and participation possible in many areas. In addition to the creation of purpose-built classrooms and speech therapy and physiotherapy rooms, a large entrance hall was built and parts of the school such as the pottery room were altered so that wheelchairs could circulate.

2.44   The new special needs department at Hirst High was part of the main building and close to the office and dining hall. Geographically, it could have been any other department in the school. Its central position could foster contact with the rest of the school. However, it was separated from the rest of the school by large double doors, put in during the renovations, as part of the attempt to give the members of the special needs department 'a secure base'. But students in wheelchairs or with other mobility problems could not go through those doors without assistance. Access for them to the rest of the school was restricted to the ground floor as there were no lifts. As we have stressed elsewhere in the course, such lack of access affects staff, parents, grandparents and other members of the community as well as students at the school who may or may not be in the special needs department.

2.45   One teacher summed up the problems posed by the building:

> We are a long way from the classrooms and the double doors prevent many of our students from circulating freely … The sixth-form block is completely isolated and students have actually got to go through three double doors to the rest of the block. We have three students in wheelchairs who would be able to get themselves there independently if there were no doors. In the old school, where all the classrooms were arranged around the hall, the students were more independent. Here their independence has gone. They've got to be pushed everywhere and sometimes you need two staff so one can open the doors. The students are aware of that. Debbie, for example, has said, 'I like the new school but I can't get around,' so she's aware that it has put constraints on her.

Participation in lessons

2.46   The way in which Michelle participated in a science lesson, as portrayed in the programme, was not typical of the way students from the special needs department shared in the academic resources of the school. In fact, a year later Michelle no longer joined in science lessons. When we were writing this, shared lessons involved five students from the department, who joined Gwen Woodman's lower-attainment year-10 option groups for English. A number of teachers did envisage greater inclusion within the lessons and not just with bottom sets. But commonly, contact with subject specialists happened when students from the department joined a member of staff in another department who was timetabled to work with them and their teachers.

2.47 Subjects such as music, pottery, sciences, technology (including home economics), PE and games were all taught by mainstream teachers to some pupils from the special needs department. These sessions were prepared jointly when possible. We observed lessons containing rich learning opportunities in which the subject specialism was central to the activity and the teaching strategies and language were adapted to meet the needs of individual students. A group of fifteen-year-olds made clocks in technology; this activity involved planning, measuring, counting, sequencing, painting and using drilling and cutting equipment. It also involved carefully focused discussion on time and time relationships. This was a technology lesson and *Blue Peter* was a thousand miles away. Hazel Coombs had been taking a group to work on forensic science, following a trail of clues in search of missing biscuits. Besides these contacts, a number of students had opted to do work experience or spend their activities week in the special needs department. But it was clear that there was a problem of continuity for some lessons, occurring once every ten-day cycle.

2.48 Janice Trotter involved a group in home economics in a certificate accreditation course. She felt that there was an overlap in attainments between her students from the special needs department and other students, but she was wary of taking groups together:

> I've done it in the past and I'm trying to work out how to do it again. At the moment I need all my energies to cope with my mainstream bottom group as a class, and I couldn't face the problem of having extra bodies.

2.49 We discussed the experience of some teachers in other schools, that having students in a group who had obvious needs for support had sometimes been found to reduce rather than exacerbate management problems.

Informal contact between students

2.50 Teachers and learning support staff seemed, in general, to feel enthusiastic about the gains made, largely through informal contact. One teacher commented:

> Their confidence is definitely up a lot because they just walk down the corridors with all the other children and the others speak to them and they'll speak back and that's given them a lot of confidence.

2.51 At the beginning of the day a small group of mainstream pupils met the young people arriving at the special needs department at Hirst High. They helped pupils out of vehicles when needed and accompanied

Pupils enjoy a maths lesson in the special needs department.

Staff at Hirst High share their knowledge and experience in different curriculum areas ...

... and pupils benefit from a wide range of equipment and a broader curriculum.

pupils in wheelchairs to their classroom. The entrance to the special needs department was at the side of the building some distance from the main entrance to the school, so pupils of the two communities arrived at the school at the same time, but entered and left through separate doors.

At the start of the school day

2.52   Dinner time was a pleasant occasion at Hirst High. The atmosphere was calm and friendly. There was no policing of behaviour, and dinner time was shared by staff, students and local retired people. The hall quickly filled up and all pupils, teachers and visitors chose where they sat, and mixed well.

Pupils from Hirst High meet those arriving at the special needs department.

Pupils arrive at the same time but enter and leave the school by different doors.

2.53   Those students from the special needs department who were able to eat independently had lunch in the school dining-room. Those students who required help in eating and most of those who used wheelchairs had their lunch separately in the special needs base. The reasons given for this arrangement were:

- the dining room would be too noisy for these pupils;
- their eating difficulties made it inappropriate for them to eat in the main dining hall because it was messy;
- too many wheelchairs would be cumbersome and block passage ways.

2.54   These views were expressed by staff who were based both inside and outside the special needs department. You may remember the lunchtime arrangements at the Grove school where all students and staff shared lunchtime, with some students being helped to eat, and this was seen as commonplace. Felicity Armstrong reported that when she was having a cup of tea and toast in the bistro, she noticed a girl from the special needs department aged about 16 giving a drink and some toast to a partially sighted boy in a wheelchair, who apparently had very little expressive language, while she talked to him. Why couldn't this boy could have his lunch in the main dining hall with similar help from other students?

2.55   The bistro was open at breaktime in the morning, when students and staff in the special needs department provided coffee and tea, hot buttered toast and biscuits. Other students were invited in, and mixed groups of pupils laughing and talking formed naturally. The numbers involved were very small because of the size of the space available and because it was felt that students from outside the department might have taken over if there was an 'open house' policy. Could a school like Hirst High contain a larger coffee bar, somewhere else in the school where all pupils could go?

2.56   Although generally students in the school had to be outside at break time and lunchtime unless it was raining, students from the special needs department were kept indoors. One lunchtime supervisor argued that there was no one designated to look after these students outside and that she and the other supervisors already had enough people to look after. At lunchtime, they could go to the youth block, play table tennis, listen to music and show off their singing talents in the karaoke. Students could also use facilities in the special needs hall which included weight training, snooker, and music. Again, other students were invited to share this time and there were six involved in various activities while we were there.

2.57   The activities going on inside and outside the school buildings at these times were things that most teenagers enjoy: hanging around in groups, laughing and talking, listening to music, playing football and

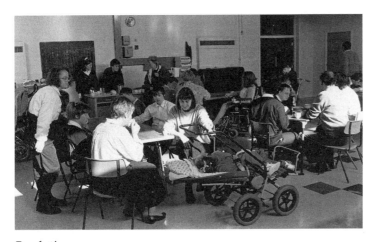

Break time.

Pupils get together in the bistro for coffee ... and a chat.

A karaoke session takes place in the youth block. Sixth formers from the special needs department sing the latest hits.

Mainstream sixth formers relax in their common area.

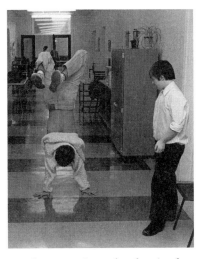

*Pupils entertain each other in the
special needs base.*

other games, looking at books, using the computer and so on. Probably
all young people enjoy at least one of these activities, they were all
available at Hirst High and yet they were not available for all the
students to enjoy together.

Contact between staff

2.58 Hirst High was a friendly community and those working there
were approachable and helpful. There was a pleasant staffroom, but
many departments had their own little 'bolt holes' close to their teaching
areas where departmental staff tended to meet for a coffee and chat at
break time. The staff from the special needs department had their own
staffroom in their base and rarely visited the main staffroom. This meant
that all the staff of the school did not meet together over coffee, on a
daily basis.

The attitude of students

2.59 Three months after we made the recordings, the students in the
special needs department appeared to have settled in and were enjoying
life at Hirst High. Some could find their way around the school
confidently and independently. Those who offered an opinion said they
liked being at Hirst High. Reasons given were 'the uniform', 'more
friends', 'better classrooms' and 'the dinners'.

2.60 We asked a number of students outside the department what they
thought about including students from the new special needs department
in tutor groups. They *all* thought this was a good idea:

> We'd get to know each other and make more friends.

> I think it would be ace. They'd settle in with us lot. They'd have a
> chance to do what we do.

I wouldn't mind. We'd get to know them and they'd get to know us. They wouldn't be frightened any more. At the beginning they'd be walking around thinking we might be laughing at them. They wouldn't be so nervous afterwards.

People would gradually accept. They wouldn't *all* accept straight away. Some would think, 'I don't know what they are doing here.' But they'd just have to get used to it, wouldn't they? I mean, it would be right different if *we* were disabled and had ability problems and that. Then *they'd* have to accept it.

2.61   On the cassette programme we heard Margaret Wells describing the students at Hirst High as 'an incredible population of children who adapt extremely well to all kinds of situations. They are patient and have a lot of humanity.' On the question of shared tutor groups for all pupils, she said:

I think it would work, not so much because of what I think or what the head thinks, or what the special needs department think but because the children of the school have always been the sort of people who would make anything work.

The views of parents

2.62   As before other similar moves, parents had been apprehensive. Katy's mother was typical in her positive view of the move once it had taken place.

I was expecting some trauma. I mean, she's a typical seventeen-year-old but with the difficulties of having a disability too. Having been in a fairly sheltered environment for most of her school years I expected the change to have quite a profound effect on her. It has, but in a much more positive way than I expected. I have to say I was very keen for this change, and I was all prepared for more difficult behaviour problems, but no. In fact, in the very short time, I've noticed she's much more mature and much more self-reliant, and her self-esteem has gone up which I think is very important.

I think it's due to a lot of things. I think it's the fact that she goes to a school where everybody else goes as well and even the very basic thing of wearing a uniform, she's quite pleased about. In some ways I've always thought uniforms made everybody look too much the same, but it's something they all seem to want to do, and I think the fact that Katy could be seen to be wearing a uniform made her feel, 'Well, I'm wearing one too.' But I think the main reason her self-esteem has gone up is that people talk about schools and she sees where everybody else goes to school. She has always thrived very much on being with other people, with other children and young people who don't necessarily have disabilities.

2.63   This parent talked about the kinds of changes she would like to see take place at Hirst High in the future and the effect the change could have on the expectations of students and parents:

> I think Katy would benefit if she could share some lessons with mainstream students in certain areas. Katy's curriculum has got to meet her needs but it's also got to open up other avenues and there are some areas that I would like to see her sharing in that way. It's early days but it is beginning to happen in a very limited way. I would like to see shared break times and shared leisure activities.

> I think parents' expectations have always been very limited, they've never thought they should have anything else ... they feel 'we should be grateful' and we've been made to feel that way as well. And really, the fact that we've made this step not only are parents' expectations raised but these students' expectations are raised. They'll want more. Not more than anybody else but just the same opportunities.

2.64   Initially information produced by the school for parents tended to omit the concerns of parents with students in the special needs department. But after parents and staff in the department had pointed this out to senior staff, procedures began to be developed to ensure that their perspective was included.

A new role for the special needs department?

2.65   After they joined the school, the staff in the special needs department continued to have responsibility for a particular group of students defined by the statementing process as having 'severe learning difficulties'. There were some indications that this responsibility was beginning to broaden. For example, two distressed homeless students had arrived at the school and, needing particular support, had started life at the school based in the department, although some staff in the department were concerned that they might be seen to have sole responsibility for all 'problematic' students and this may reduce the involvement of other members of staff.

2.66   The skills that department staff had to offer students across the school in a variety of curriculum areas were also recognized. There was a suggestion that learning support as a whole could be seen as emanating from the department and that this could come to define a new broader role in the school. As Gwen Woodman acknowledged in response to this suggestion:

> That would be wonderful. That would seem to me some kind of ultimate goal that they should be seen as the people that help to support every child in the school who has difficulties at the start, and then go on from there.

Including some, excluding others?

2.67   The presence in the school of some students who had statements specifying a category of 'learning difficulty', prompts questions about the absence of others. Students who were perceived as being more able than the students in the special needs department but who were categorized as having 'moderate learning difficulties' were sent to a special school in Morpeth. It would be hard to provide a legal defence of that practice if parents appealed against it, given the provision available in the mainstream at Hirst High and at the middle and first school. But the head was wary that an increase in numbers of students perceived as having difficulties at the school might detract from the image of the school as concerned with achievement.

2.68   And what of other disabled students? Could the school support students who are physically disabled or are deaf? Could it have a policy of including all students within its communities, irrespective of attainment or disability?

CONCLUSION: ENHANCING PARTICIPATION FOR ALL?

2.69   As one way of documenting the response of Hirst High to the diversity of its students, we examined the way students were divided into groups on the basis of their attainments and presumed ability. One consequence of this system is that it exaggerated the labelling of students as clever or not, and separated them socially. There was a further by-product of this classification system in the dramatic gender imbalance within attainment sets and the considerable problems of participation in the curriculum for boys that this represented.

2.70   The study of grouping, as well as of the timetabling policies, helped us to make sense of the possibilities for, and progress in, the inclusion of students from Riverbank Special School. Hirst High School was in the very early stages of combining two populations of staff and students. Already, great changes had taken place in the lives of the relatively small number of students and staff who had come from Riverbank school. The changes for the large number of students and staff who were already at the school had been fewer. How would you like to see the school develop?

Activity 3   How could the participation of students be enhanced?

If we want to increase the participation of students in the social and learning opportunities at this school, we have to identify current differences in participation and possibilities for enhancing it. Make a list of the aspects of the school that you might wish to look at in order to enhance student participation.

2.71 We made this list:

1 How are student achievements represented, for example in the entrance to the school and in the literature produced by it?

2 What could be done to reduce pressure for setting and the gender imbalance between sets?

3 What could be done to improve the involvement of boys in the school and reduce the problems of control they are seen to present?

4 Could there be a return to in-class support rather than a fifth 'remedial' set?

5 Could more of the students categorized as having severe learning difficulties who now attend Hirst High School take up their right to attend their *neighbourhood schools*?

6 Could students categorized as having moderate learning difficulties (currently excluded from the school) be encouraged to attend it?

7 Could all students from the area irrespective of disability or attainment be offered a place at this school?

8 Could all students share the same school entrances and lunch and break arrangements?

   Could students categorized as having severe learning difficulties attend tutor groups and share more academic activities?

10 How could barriers to physical access to the school be reduced?

11 How could social training opportunities of staff be widened?

12 How could the activities of the special needs department and learning support staff be more closely co-ordinated?

'Sir, we won two nil!'

3 CONTROLLING CHANGE

3.1   The teachers at Hirst High were attempting to control the way their school developed while outside pressures forced their hands. In particular, they faced cuts in their budget and rising unemployment in their area. They were also in the throes of introducing the national curriculum and responding to the pressure to be competitive resulting from the 1988 Education Act, and these have intensified with the 1993 Education Act. In this section we will set out:

- the information which school governors must make available to parents;
- how the process of creating a formal school development plan can help teachers to give priority to their own principles while accommodating legislation which may spring from others.

We then analyse the views of some people working in special schools with a range of visions of the future. We provide two examples of changes to special schools which were instigated by their own staff and supported by LEAs.

DESCRIBING SCHOOLS

3.2   All schools have to provide a description of their activities in a school prospectus and in an annual governors' report and have to make available for inspection by parents their curriculum policies, schemes of work and the government documents regulating them. The information to be contained in a prospectus is summarized in Figure 1 (p. 30), and we have italicized those items where there is most opportunity to indicate how a school responds to diversity. While the special education policy has to be available as 'a single document' and may therefore encourage a view of difficulties in learning as something separate, it is clearly possible for teachers to share and report a view of learning and difficulties in learning which is concerned with the development and participation of all students.

3.3   The annual governors' report must include very detailed information about 'special educational provision', 'identification, assessment and provision for pupils with special educational needs' and information about 'staffing policies' and 'partnership' with others outside the school. This information required is set out in Appendix A to the supplement to Unit 1/2 (*How Should We React to Government Policies? Responding to the Code of Practice*, pp. 21–23) and differs considerably among mainstream, special and hospital special schools. As described in Unit 14/15, the 1995 Disability Discrimination Act has added, apparently, three further requirements to the list:

(a) the arrangements for the admission of disabled pupils;

(b) the steps taken to prevent disabled pupils from being treated less favourably than other pupils; and

(c) the facilities provided to assist access to the school by disabled pupils.

(Disability Discrimination Act 1995, Section 29)

3.4   Figure 2 (p. 31) sets out the information required from mainstream schools. If you look at item 6 you can see that the third point in the quotation from the 1995 Disability Discrimination Act was already required, but has been given added significance by the way disability is defined in the Act (which further complicated the definitions of learning difficulty and special need in the 1993 Education Act and the Code of Practice). When Tony Booth discussed the definitions in Unit 1/2, he treated 'disability' as if it was relatively unproblematic, assuming that those framing legislation related disability to an underlying physical impairment. However, the definition of disability in the 1995 Act includes both 'mental impairment' and 'physical impairment':

> A person has a disability for the purposes of this Act if he has a physical or mental impairment which has a substantial and long-term adverse effect on his ability to carry out normal day-to-day activities.

3.5   A 'mental impairment' is not further explained but presumably is a reason for low attainment or learning difficulty as officially defined. Thus, in asking schools how they propose to admit disabled students and to support them, the 1995 Disability Discrimination Act gives a clear direction to schools to include students who experience 'substantial and long-term' difficulties in learning which are such as to make 'normal' day-to-day activities problematic. This must include students categorized as having 'severe learning difficulties' as well as any lesser degree of difficulty.

Activity 4   From special needs to learning for all

Look at the information presented in Schedule 1 of the 1994 Regulations in Figure 2, add the requirements of the 1995 Disability Discrimination Act (as quoted in para. 3.3 above), and rewrite the list as a series of questions about overcoming the difficulties in learning experienced by any student in a school, rather than a group categorized as having 'special needs'. This requires two shifts of focus: from a narrow to a broader group of students and from identifying difficulties in students to improving teaching and learning relationships and resources. You may end up with fewer or more points and may have to decide how radically you wish to depart from the official list.

Figure 1   Information concerning the curriculum for inclusion in school prospectuses (adapted from Harris, 1995, p. 154).

Name, address, telephone number of school.

Names of head teacher and chair of governors.

Classification of the school (county/voluntary aided etc.; primary, middle or secondary; comprehensive, secondary modern, grammar or bilateral; co-educational or single-sex; etc.)

Admissions policy

Arrangements for visits by parents of prospective pupils.

Secondary schools: number of places for pupils at normal age of entry; number of written applications or expressions of preference for places.

Statement on curriculum and organisation of education and teaching methods at the school, including special arrangements for statemented pupils and others and a summary of the 'special educational needs policy'.

A statement on 'the ethos and values of the school'.

In the case of any county, voluntary or maintained special school (other than a special school established in a hospital) information on the procedure for curriculum etc. complaints under section 23 of the ERA 1988.

A summary of the content and organization of sex education.

Particulars of careers guidance and arrangements for work experience (if any).

Religious affiliation of the school, if any, and particulars of religious education and parental right to withdraw their child from it.

A summary of charging policy and policy on remission of charges.

Dates of school holidays, including half-term holidays; and the times at which each school session begins and ends on a school day.

Changes relating to any of the above as compared with the previous year.

Prescribed information on the level of attainment of pupils in national curriculum subjects, and in some cases, local and national averages; in a secondary school, prescribed information on GCSE, A/AS level and vocational qualification results and the destinations of pupils who have left (e.g. employment, further or higher education, training etc.).

In Wales, particulars of the Welsh language at the school.

Information about the level of unauthorized absences of pupils.

Figure 2 Information required of county, voluntary and grant-maintained schools (Schedule 1 of the Education (Special Educational Needs) (Information) Regulations 1994, in Circular 6/94, DfEE, 1994).

Basic information about the school's special educational provision

1   The objectives of the governing body in making provision for pupils with special educational needs, and a description of how the governing body's special educational needs policy will contribute towards meeting those objectives.

2   The name of the person who is responsible for co-ordinating the day to day provision of education for pupils with special educational needs at the school (whether or not the person is known as the SEN co-ordinator).

3   The arrangements which have been made for co-ordinating the provision of education for pupils with special educational needs at the school.

4   The admission arrangements for pupils with special educational needs who do not have a statement in so far as they differ from the arrangements for other pupils.

5   The kinds of provision for special educational needs in which the school specialises and any special units.

6   Facilities for pupils with special educational needs at the school including facilities which increase or assist access to the school by pupils who are disabled.

Information about the school's policies for the identification, assessment and provision for all pupils with special educational needs

7   How resources are allocated to and amongst pupils with special educational needs.

8   How pupils with special educational needs are identified and their needs determined and reviewed.

9   Arrangements for providing access by pupils with special educational needs to a balanced and broadly based curriculum (including the National Curriculum).

10 How pupils with special educational needs engage in the activities of the school together with pupils who do not have special educational needs.

11 How the governing body evaluate the success of the education which is provided at the school to pupils with special educational needs.

12 Any arrangements made by the governing body relating to the treatment of complaints from parents of pupils with special educational needs concerning the provision made at the school.

Information about the school's staffing policies and partnership with bodies beyond the school

13 Any arrangements made by the governing body relating to in-service training for staff in relation to special educational needs.

14 The use made of teachers and facilities from outside the school including links with support services for special educational needs.

15 The role played by the parents of pupils with special educational needs.

16 Any links with other schools, including special schools, and the provision made for the transition of pupils with special educational needs between schools or between the school and the next stage of life or education.

17 Links with child health services, social services and educational welfare services and any voluntary organisations which work on behalf of children with special educational needs.

3.6 We have set out below our attempt to do Activity 4. In order to relate this list to the way difficulties in learning and 'special needs' are usually defined, we would include a few brief cameos of difficulties identified, supported or overcome. These would be fictionalized and would have to involve a fair degree of diplomacy towards teachers, parents and students. We have mapped the official list onto our questions by including the list's numbers in brackets at the end of each question.

SCHOOL POLICY ON DIFFICULTIES IN LEARNING

1   What difficulties in learning are experienced by students? How are these identified? What policies are in place to reduce or prevent them? How is the success of these policies monitored? (1, 8, 3, 11, 9)

2   Who is responsible for co-ordinating the reduction of difficulties in learning and promoting learning development? (2)

3   What resources and expertise are available at the school to reduce difficulties in learning and support disabled students? How can these be increased? (5, 6, 7, 13)

4   What resources and expertise are used from beyond the school, including collaboration with other schools and agencies? (6, 7, 14, 16, 17)

5   Are all students in the neighbourhood encouraged to enrol at the school (irrespective of disability and attainment)? How does the school attempt to reduce barriers to their attendance and participation in learning and social activities? (4, (a) and (b) in para. 3.3 above, 9)

6   What is done to minimize selection within the school? (10)

7   How are parents involved in improving teaching and learning at the school and how can they raise concerns about difficulties in learning experienced by their children? (15, 12)

8   How are students involved in identifying and overcoming difficulties in learning?

9   What is done to minimize the difficulties experienced by students when they leave the school? (16)

FORMAL SCHOOL PLANS

3.7 From whatever direction outside pressures come, it is important for those working in schools who wish to control their destinies to devise their own plans for development. In the case of Hirst High we saw that the suggestions from some teachers, that there should be an explicit plan for incorporating ex-Riverbank students into the heart of school life, was not supported by management. We have suggested that the requirements for the presentation of information by governors is best seen as part of a development plan for teaching, learning and resources in the school as a whole, although a document related to issues of 'special needs' has to be available as a 'single document'. Here we examine the process of creating a school development plan.

Activity 5 Planning school development

Christine Gilbert, director of education in the London Borough of Harrow, was formerly head of Whitmore School which was described and discussed in Unit 1/2. She wrote a chapter for us on school development plans called 'Planning school development', which is Chapter 3 in Reader 2. A development plan for Whitmore High School is used as an example in that chapter. It is a detailed chapter, with some education jargon, and how much you want to go into its details may depend on your position within education. At the most general level, when you have read it you should have a reasonably clear idea about how you would set about co-ordinating a development plan for a primary or secondary school, either of which may be a special school, and perhaps be able to think how the principles might be applied to a nursery school or further education college. It may help you to consider the following questions as you read the chapter.

- How would you convince a group of staff that a formal development plan was a good idea?

- What stages would you go through when drawing up a plan?

- Who would you involve?

- How would you determine the priorities for the short and long term?

3.8   We do not intend to repeat the detail of the chapter here but to emphasize two points. It is striking how the complexity of the planning process increases with the size of the school and is a feature of secondary rather than primary schools. Any shared development plan for a further education college or a university would be extremely difficult to achieve. Christine Gilbert also stresses that the process of producing the plan is as important as its content:

> ... joint ownership of the plan not only gives the school a clearer and more united sense of purpose, but also reduces the stress generated by the speed and extent of educational changes.

(Reader 2, p. 69)

3.9   We do not need to remind you that the writers of this course have not taken a neutral line about the inclusion within the mainstream of students who experience difficulties or have disabilities. We set out our aims in the *Course Guide* and two of the aims specifically encourage the process of integration:

- To enable students to facilitate a process of increasing the inclusion and participation of pupils from special schools and separate units within mainstream groups.

- To encourage the development of teaching methods and curricula which support the shared learning of diverse groups.

(*Course Guide*, p. 5)

3.10   Because of our aims and the principles that underlie them, there has been an emphasis on examples of mainstream practice in the course and we know that at some points this has left some of you feeling less than fully included. We want you all to feel valued as learners, but does the emphasis on mainstream schools and colleges mean that the work of some course participants is devalued? That is not our intention. We know that there are excellent staff and excellent lessons in special schools. But we would not wish to slide out of controversy by coming up with the often repeated diplomatic formula that 'special schools do an excellent job and there will always be a place for them' (see Unit 10). This leaves open the question of whether the segregated sector should be greater or smaller than it is at present. Nor would we wish to encourage the simplistic opinion that all or most of those working in special schools oppose integration. As will be clear from this unit and elsewhere in the course many of the most imaginative and forceful ideas about integration have emerged from special schools. If we are true to our principles then we have to spell out that we would like to see very few students educated outside the mainstream. An appropriately resourced and supported mainstream would include virtually all those at present in special schools. This is not an idealistic option but a logical consequence of examining real possibilities for the inclusion of students in the mainstream.

3.11   The examples provided in this unit, in addition to those elsewhere in the course, should help you to reflect on the extent to which you agree with us. We think that it is not sensible to attempt to run both an integrated and segregated system with the distribution to be determined by choices of parents and students and the vagaries of professional opinion, partly because to run two systems is an expensive option. We argue that where the reallocation of resources is carefully planned, an integrated system need be no more expensive than one relying on the continuation of special schools (see Audit Commission/HMI, 1992a). Students at the Grove School were supported, for example, with resource reallocated from the special school budget. In moving from one system to the other, however, there are start-up costs, for example in adapting buildings and duplicating staff and resources (see Coopers and Lybrand, 1992). But the main reason for making a policy choice is that the principles underlying the two systems send incompatible messages to mainstream schools. The maintenance of a selective approach undermines an inclusive one. But where special schools do remain there can be little justification for continuing with compulsory segregation. Would special schools survive if parents could not be compelled to send their students there and could expect to gain the same level of resource to support their children within the mainstream?

3.12   At an E242 day school in Cambridge, some students opened a discussion about how these issues were considered within the course. With one student, Jo Koegel, who is deaf and works with young people who are deaf and blind, this discussion continued by fax. She was doing E242 as part of an advanced diploma in health and social welfare, having already studied the *Issues of Deafness* course. Another student, Sally Davies, who works in a school for students categorized as having 'moderate learning difficulties', set down her concerns in a letter. She wrote when she had finished Unit 8/9 and perhaps her thoughts would have been different if she had read further units. She felt at the time that the course undervalued the contribution of special school staff to the education of young people. Here is her letter:

> In the *Course Guide* for E242 *Learning for All* one of the stated aims is:
>
>> To enable students to understand the system of education and special education.
>
> In order to do this I feel that students must be presented with a clear, balanced view of what exists at the present time in the world of special education. An explanation of the variety of schools would be appropriate. Whilst many students may be aware of schools that cater for physical or mental disabilities, are they also aware of the schools which are termed MLD or EBD? Are they aware of the role that these schools play or is the course presenting them as devalued aspects of education? The course materials have made references to such schools – Unit 6/7's descriptions of mathematical activities and a collaborative learning project, for example, both serve to illustrate styles of teaching which are normal practice in special schools but this is not necessarily the impression given.
>
> Throughout the course materials there is a great emphasis on integration of pupils who experience difficulties or have disabilities and on methods by which successful integration can be achieved. Where in this course are students told about the success and achievements made in MLD and EBD schools? These schools also have 'values' in education and are acutely aware of the need for socialization and emotional as well as physical development. Indeed it is often these schools which are better able to adapt circumstances to allow and promote such development in a way which is more structured towards the needs of the particular child and which is

less threatening than the approach and atmosphere to which some pupils are exposed in some examples of integration. Not all segregation is a failure and not all integration is a success.

The course places integration in direct opposition to segregation, seeing it as the only solution to the problem of creating an education system that is open and fair to all. To integrate pupils in mainstream schools does not necessarily mean greater achievement, adjustment or equality. It is very difficult to make it work, it is not a cheap option and it is fraught with political problems. Will the course discuss or make allowance for the financial and political decisions which are not made by teachers?

Finally, if students following this course are to be given the opportunity to reflect on the impact of the National Curriculum on children who experience difficulties, does Will Swann's chapter 'Hardening the hierarchies' [Reader 1, Chapter 7] provide a balanced view? Whilst I would agree that not everything about the NC is perfect I feel that it has opened up new opportunities for curriculum discussion and the sharing of resources between schools not just between special and mainstream schools but also between infant, junior, primary and secondary phases.

If E242 *Learning for All* is to mean 'all', then I feel that the course must examine educational practice as it exists today. Integration is one aspect of this practice and segregation is another. One of the other tasks should be how to make both valued elements of the system and not to promote prejudice or disaffection and certainly not to promote the one at the expense of the valuable and principled work done by the other.

Sally Davies

3.13 The categories of special school are outlined in the supplement to Unit 1/2 (*How Should We React to Government Policies? Responding to the Code of Practice*). The provision for students categorized as having 'emotional and behavioural difficulties' is discussed in Unit 11/12. However, it is true that nowhere in the course is there as detailed a picture of what goes on inside a special school as those of the Grove or Whitmore in Unit 1/2 or Hirst High in the previous section of this unit, although Tim Southgate does redress this to some extent later in this section.

3.14 We think that good teaching occurs in a wide variety of places, inside and outside schools. Sally Davies feels that teachers in special schools may be especially adept at responding to the particular needs of individuals and providing a 'less threatening' atmosphere. We argue that you can find responsive teachers and confident students, who have experienced difficulties in learning, within both mainstream and special schools. We also point to the contradiction in special schools grouping students according to categories of disability or inability and then attempting to respond to them 'as individuals'. Sally Davies seems to believe that we are suggesting that 'all segregation is a failure' and 'all integration is a success'. We do not see it in those terms. We feel that each of us needs to come to a carefully considered view about the system of education we would prefer, recognizing that any human system will have its share of success and failure. The view we have come to, is that a system which works towards inclusion and participation and against exclusion is to be preferred to one in which present levels of exclusion are encouraged or increased. Sally Davies feels that we should not promote one approach 'at the expense of the valuable and principled work done by the other'. We argue that it would be dishonest not to follow through the clear implications of our principles and the aims for this course.

3.15   Sally Davies also makes a point about Will Swann's view of the national curriculum (revised according to the Dearing recommendations as discussed in Unit 14/15) and the positive effect she feels that the national curriculum has had on broadening discussion of the curriculum and on the sharing of resources. We recognize the positive effects that national curriculum discussions have made to the breadth of the curriculum (a point made by Will Swann, Reader 1, p. 86, third paragraph). In raising the spectre of exemptions, it has brought out into the open, too, a shared view within mainstream and special schools that all students have an entitlement to broad curricular opportunities.

Activity 6   Changing places

Chapter 4 in Reader 2 is about the developments that have taken place in a special school in Oxford and the way it supports its students. It is written by the head teacher, Tim Southgate, who became an enthusiastic supporter of integration for most disabled students and of separate conductive education for some. Many of the issues it raises were brought to your attention in previous units, particularly Units 1/2, 8/9 and Unit 10. As you read the chapter you might consider the following questions:

- What was the rationale for grouping disabled students together at Ormerod School in the early 1980s?

- How was integration based on the needs of students?

- How important for the successful participation of disabled students was the statement of principles by the head teacher of Marlborough Comprehensive School?

- To what extent do you agree with the idea of grouping students together for conductive education in a community separated from the mainstream?

3.16   The chapter describes the way Tim Southgate and the Ormerod staff collaborated with mainstream schools to promote the integration of students. Oxfordshire allowed individual schools the autonomy to develop in this way before local management of schools, and Ormerod was sufficiently well resourced to initiate the necessary adaptations to buildings. Bureaucratic hurdles were minimal. The changes in the school fitted into a local authority policy encouraging integration, though not in a highly co-ordinated fashion (see Jones, 1983; Sayer, 1987; CSIE, 1992).

3.17   When Tim Southgate became head teacher of Ormerod he inherited a special school which contained students sent there because of physical disability. It might seem that there was an educational principle, albeit a mistaken one, underlying such a practice; that students with a category of disability in common were seen to require common curricula or teaching methods. However, as Tim Southgate explains, in schools for students categorized by disability there may be a wider range of attainment and interest than is found in most mainstream schools. The classification is medical and administrative rather than educational.

3.18   Tim Southgate argues that:

> The school has been led throughout by the needs of the children and as these needs have changed or the perception or understanding of them has altered so the school has responded by creating new structures and developing new approaches.

But according to Tim Southgate himself, Ormerod School was set up to cater for a category of disability rather than the educational needs of its students. And if it was not set up according to 'need', could it be dismantled according to 'need'? A pragmatic response to the circumstances he inherited seems to be represented here as being 'led throughout by the needs of the children'.

3.19   The concept of need is problematic, in itself, as was pointed out at the start of the course and discussed in Unit 10. The needs of students are usually defined by other people. This further reduces the force of Tim Southgate's concern that integration should be seen as a response to need, rather than as a human right or 'an end in itself'. We are not sure what seeing integration 'as an end in itself' means. We suspect that he is arguing that an integrated system is not to be preferred to a segregated one on moral grounds as good, or preferable 'in itself'. He differs then from the writers of this course who argue for the moral desirability of an inclusive system in which the diversity of students is celebrated and students learn co-operatively together irrespective of their attainments or disabilities. Equally we argue that a comprehensive, community-oriented system of nursery, primary and secondary schools and ultimately and ideally further and higher education, is to be preferred to a system selecting by attainment, disability or wealth. This preference is based on a view of the society we would like for ourselves and our children. It makes little sense to suggest that a comprehensive and selective system should exist in parallel or even less that the choice between the systems can be based on need. Although we argue for this system this does not mean that we demand that others share our perspective. We ask only that others analyse the moral or social principles as well as the pragmatic and practical considerations which underlie their choices.

3.20   Do children and young people have a *right* to attend a mainstream school or their local school? Do parents have a *right* to be able to send them to one? We argue that students do have the right to attend their local school but that this right may conflict in extreme cases with the rights of others to learn or work free from intimidation or violence. Unit 11/12 looked at issues of control and disaffection and you will be aware of the complexity of the causes of disruption in schools and what can be done to minimize it. People also have the right to form groups based on culture, identity and interest. But Tim Southgate does not make a distinction between such voluntary separation and the compulsory segregation that can be an outcome of the statementing process. *We see compulsory segregation as an infringement of human rights.*

3.21   Gerry O'Hagan, who was head of Marlborough school when students from Ormerod started moving there, did not think that his school had 'a right to refuse any child from [the] catchment area if the parent wanted the child to attend' (Reader 2, p. 73). Although Tim Southgate does not recognize this right he seemed to regard the principle as of great significance in easing the process of inclusion of his students. Of course, people can state one set of principles while basing their practice on another set entirely. It is actions and the often implicit principles which underlie them which are more important than rhetoric. In the case of Marlborough school, it seems that the principles were stated *and* acted upon.

3.22   Marlborough was not the local school for many of the disabled students and the Ormerod staff showed an unusual degree of flexibility in starting and adapting schemes so that more students could attend their neighbourhood schools. This local initiative was able to create a more sophisticated model of integration than common in many LEAs, where advisers may act as if the task of promoting integration is over once a mainstream school has been resourced to include a group of students from a special school.

3.23   The Ormerod model conformed more closely to our view of integration as a never-ending process of increasing the participation of students in the educational and social life of mainstream schools and communities and reducing exclusionary pressures. When thought of in this way, integration involves all students and merges with the ideals of comprehensive, community, lifelong education. Integration, like democracy, involves an unending series of steps bringing people greater knowledge and control of the decisions and social practices which affect their lives. This is a further meaning that can be given to rejecting integration as 'an end in itself'.

3.24   But links for students between special and mainstream schools have sometimes been put into practice as if any contact must be good 'in itself'. Thus at one special school at which Tony Booth was a governor, a particular student was attending four mainstream schools 'for integration' as well as his special school. In his governor's report, he suggested that given the incredible flexibility that was expected of this student in adapting to five schools perhaps he should go to only one mainstream school, but attend it full-time.

3.25 Ormerod transmuted, finally, into a school for students with a narrower range of ages and disabilities who followed a curriculum based on conductive education. The numbers were back up to the levels of the early 1980s. Given the narrowed range, some of these students must have travelled even greater distances than those who had attended the special school, previously. The arguments surrounding conductive education were considered in Unit 8/9 and we will not repeat them here. But if the special school had not already been in existence, would we have set up a conductive education group away from the mainstream?

Activity 7 Moving on, moving in and moving out

Even greater changes were taking place at another special school in Oxfordshire in the 1980s. Roger Kidd, then head of Bishopswood School for students categorized as having severe learning difficulties, worked with his staff and collaborating mainstream schools, with support from the LEA, to transfer the children and young people from his school into the mainstream. He left the school to take up a post as head of Etton Pasture Special School for students categorized as having 'moderate learning difficulties' in the East Riding area of Humberside, and repeated the Bishopswood formula over a four-year period there. Chapter 5 in Reader 2 is his description of the way the students and resources were transferred from his school into the mainstream. As you read the chapter you might consider the following issues:

- To what extent are the approaches to change developed within one LEA relevant to a different one?

- What justifications are there for maintaining special schools for students categorized as having moderate learning difficulties?

- To what extent would you wish to include approaches to difficulties in learning and behaviour within a single policy?

- What are the advantages and disadvantages of basing a learning support service within the special education sector of an LEA rather than in particular schools?

3.26 When Roger Kidd moved to Humberside he found that initially he had less scope for contributing to changes in policy than he had had in Oxfordshire. However, the preparation of an LEA-wide strategy meant that, overall, the reduction of segregation might be more far-reaching. There was a clear recognition within the plan that integration was a continuing process that did not stop once students were attached to a resource base within a mainstream school.

3.27 Roger Kidd had been convinced by his experience at Bishopswood school that if students categorized as having severe learning difficulties could be in the mainstream then there could be no justification for excluding students said to have moderate learning difficulties. He was determined that they should receive the same level of support within the mainstream as they received in Etton Pasture. Continuity of support was assured when he became head of the East Riding support service.

3.28   However, the education of students who had acquired the label of having 'emotional and behavioural difficulties' was not part of the LEA integration plan. When Etton Pasture closed, it reopened as a redesignated special school and five of the teachers opted to stay on. The new school allowed some students to be educated within Humberside who had previously been sent out to residential provision. However, given the pressures in the 1990s to exclude students seen to be difficult in behaviour that were documented in Unit 11/12, it is likely that the filling of one special school will do little to relieve them. An opportunity was lost, perhaps temporarily, to bring together policies about difficulties in learning and behaviour. Given that inappropriate curricula can lead to disaffection and disruption, then it is always possible that students coming out of the special school they had attended because of experiencing learning difficulties in the mainstream might return there under a new title of having 'emotional and behavioural difficulties'. A growing segregated sector for students said to have emotional and behavioural difficulties is a discouragement to schools to make connections between difficulties in learning, behaviour and control.

3.29   Humberside has gone down the route of developing a large support service, funded by the LEA special education budget, with some staff based in mainstream and others working peripatetically. Such services are vulnerable to cuts, particularly since models of funding are now based on individual mainstream or special schools. These problems were discussed in Unit 14/15, particularly in relation to the Staffordshire learning support service (see Chapter 34 in Reader 2). In the absence of very clear and effective co-ordinating powers over special education outside and within the mainstream, LEAs are caught between two alternatives. Do they retain support teachers and hope that schools will pay for them or do they devolve them to schools and hope that schools will continue to give students who experience difficulties a sufficient degree of priority?

4 A COMMON CONCERN

4.1   The course has covered a wide area and some students have written to us or told us that they would have liked greater concentration on some of the topics. But this broad area also creates problems of definition. What do all the areas of study that we have placed together have in common? What unites discussion of policies for the under-fives in Unit 5, of truancy in Unit 11/12, of power and influence in education in Unit 14/15, and of the language of instruction in producing and preventing difficulties in learning in Unit 6/7? After all, the concerns of the course seem to cover the whole of education rather than a segment of it.

4.2   We have a number of connected ideas for drawing our field of study together. We share a common concern to reduce or prevent the difficulties, of learning or participation, that children and young people experience in education. *We see the project of this course as a shared attempt to describe and understand the education system from the perspective of students who experience difficulties or experience exclusion from full participation in the educational and social life of mainstream schools and colleges.* It is a position of understanding of, or advocacy for, or alliance with, students who experience difficulties or devaluation or have disabilities. It is our method for beginning to reduce the difficulties faced by students.

4.3   In attempting to make sense of the world of education from the perspective of those who have difficulties in it, in trying to remove barriers to learning and participation, we develop a critique of education. We argue that this critique is valuable for the whole of the education system since it is concerned with the development of an approach to education that is appropriate for all students.

4.4   Does a shared interest in reducing the difficulties students encounter commit us to a common set of principles to inform our practice? In his survey of mainstream 'special needs' practice, Alan Dyson (1992) has distinguished between 'state of the art' good practice in schools and 'innovatory practice' which is said to be at the cutting edge of transformations of learning support and development. The notions of 'good practice' or 'state of the art practice' or 'innovatory practice' presume a common purpose. Yet what is good or innovatory for some, may be anathema to others. In 1992, Goebbels' diaries were serialized in the *Sunday Times*. The innovatory solution to diversity associated with Goebbels is not part of what most of us would regard as good practice. What other practices does our common concern exclude?

4.5   At various points in the course, we have discussed two opposing solutions to teaching the diversity of students in schools which can be called 'selective' and 'inclusive'. Each is informed by a set of moral and political values which in turn limits the approaches to reducing difficulties in schools, to raising standards. The selective approach starts from the assumption that learning takes place best in groups of 'similar' learners and involves a search for ways of selecting and matching students, methods, curricula and schools. It assumes further that the process and prospect of selection provide incentives to try harder and disincentives to falling behind.

4.6   We have argued that selection and segregation are inevitably bound up with the ascription of differences in worth to students on the basis of background, attainment and disability. The devaluation of students creates a pool of potential disaffection which contributes to difficulties in learning. If it contributes to devaluation and difficulties in learning, the selective approach conflicts with our common concern.

4.7   But we have to recognize that practice is often informed by a mass of conflicting principles emerging from ourselves or others with authority over us, which push in opposing directions. For example, rigid setting arrangements may be created alongside an attempt to value the diversity of backgrounds and attainments of all students. Such opposing forces were evident at Hirst High School. However, it seems to surprise some people that practices should be chosen because of principle. For example, Trevor Payne has questioned the preoccupation with in-class support rather than withdrawal in the following way:

> With very few exceptions, readers and audiences were exhorted to embrace the concept of in-class support for children with learning difficulties as a *fait accompli*, as an almost moral and social imperative. Those teachers still daring to actually withdraw children from their mainstream classes for 'remedial tuition' (both unfashionable words) must have felt like accomplices to some form of educational apartheid.
>
> (Payne, 1992, p. 61)

4.8   As we have argued in Units 1/2 and 6/7, Trevor Payne is right in drawing attention to a real problem. Some teachers do avoid withdrawal because they think it is frowned upon. But he misunderstands the source of the difficulty. It usually arises because the relationship between principles and practices is left unstated. In-class support is promoted, at least in part, because when used effectively it can help to promote inclusive classroom strategies for differentiating curricula. Withdrawal is rejected as a general solution to resolving difficulties in learning because it helps to support the myth of homogeneity; that most students require the same approach and content in their lessons, which in turn promotes inflexible teaching.

4.9   It is clear that the circumstances in which principles are applied change dramatically. Central and local government policies and changes in the level of resources create a kaleidoscope of shifting contexts. In several areas at the moment cuts in local budgets have led to the threat of the sudden withdrawal of support for some students in the mainstream. In other areas mainstream support has never materialized and parents are asking LEAs to provide special school placements as a result (*Guardian Education*, 16 March 1993, p. 2). A shift to more subject-based teaching in classes divided by attainment has been urged for primary schools and the provision of different standard attainment tasks for students according to curriculum level is pushing those secondary schools which have retained mixed-ability groups to move towards a greater use of sets (*The Times Educational Supplement*, 19 March 1993, p. 5).

4.10   Priorities about which difficulties should receive our attention change. New priorities may be a product of changing policies or may force themselves on us through media and other social pressures. As priorities change it is inevitable that the work of those in the system who concern themselves with difficulties in schools will also change. Unit 1/2 refers to the (as yet) small number of children in the UK who are infected with HIV or are affected by having a family member with HIV or AIDS. Unit 11/12 documents a growing concern with bullying and sexual and racial harassment.

4.11   Change which should have taken place in some areas of practice has been limited. The rigid demarcation which still exists in some schools between those who are meant to respond to difficulties of behaviour and control and those who busy themselves with supporting learning makes little theoretical or practical sense. The major impact teachers can make in reducing disaffection in schools is through the curriculum, just as it is for preventing and reducing difficulties in learning.

4.12   We have still a long way to go, too, before there is an acceptance of diversity in the sexual orientation of students. About 10 per cent of young people grow up as gay or lesbian. They often feel a sense of exclusion which may interfere with learning in school. We think that we should accept and value the diversity of students as good in itself, not because it may raise attainment levels. But showing how the devaluation of or low expectations for students can lead to disaffection and underachievement provides an added reason to place the valuing of diversity at the centre of our common concern.

4.13   In this course we have argued that a clear and explicit set of principles should inform an approach to diversity in schools. Differences in principle may lead to conflict but the belief that education changes through consensus is false. It enables those with power to reduce opposition to their policies. The reaction of some to the illusion of consultation before the 1988 Education Act or the 1993 Education Act can be likened to a Thurber cartoon. It depicts two fencers. One of them cries 'Touché!' as he swings and cuts off the head of the other. There is a look of affront and recrimination in the eyes of the severed head at this breach of etiquette. But it is too late.

Touché!

4.14   However, there are signs that the movement towards more selective and competitive schools, which promote failure as a necessary side-effect of success, may falter in the long term. The rise in the numbers of temporary and permanent exclusions may yet point to a politically unacceptable result of selective policies within schools. And can politicians of any political party continue to ignore the crucial role that neighbourhood schools can play in regenerating and sustaining communities, particularly in the inner cities? But a main cause for our optimism is that people do not want their local school to become extinct in the struggle for survival. Most parents and students want a good neighbourhood school. For the writers of this course, a good local school is one that serves and values all the members of its communities.

4.15 We have chosen to end the course, as we started it with an image of an assembly. In November 1992, Dorothy Bordass, who created the lithograph of *Midsummer Fair* that serves as the cover image of celebration and inclusion for this course, died aged 85. It seemed appropriate to finish the course with her image of a theatre audience. For us it symbolizes an assembly of diversity.

Audience *by Dorothy Bordass, lithograph.*

REFERENCES

AUDIT COMMISSION/HMI (1992a) *Getting in on the Act: provision for pupils with special educational needs*, London, HMSO.

AUDIT COMMISSION/HMI (1992b) *Getting the Act Together: a management handbook for schools and local education authorities*, London, HMSO.

BOOTH, T. and JONES, A. (1987) 'Extending primary practice' in BOOTH, T., POTTS, P. and SWANN, W. (eds) *Curricula for All: preventing difficulties in learning*, Oxford, Blackwell/The Open University.

CENTRE FOR STUDIES OF INTEGRATION IN EDUCATION (CSIE) (1992) *Bishopswood: good practice transferred*, London, CSIE.

COOPERS AND LYBRAND (1992) *Within Reach: access for disabled children to mainstream education*, London, the National Union of Teachers and the Spastics Society.

DEPARTMENT FOR EDUCATION (DFE) (1992a) *Choice and Diversity: a new framework for schools*, London, HMSO.

DEPARTMENT FOR EDUCATION (DFE) (1992b) *Exclusions: a discussion paper*, London, HMSO.

DYSON, A. (1992) 'Innovatory mainstream practice: what's happening in schools' provision for special needs?', *Support for Learning*, 7(2), pp. 51–57

HARRIS, N. (1995) *The Law Relating to Schools*, Croydon, Tolley.

JONES, N. (1983) 'The management of integration: the Oxfordshire experience' in Booth, T. and Potts, P. (eds) *Integrating Special Education*, Oxford, Blackwell/The Open University.

JUPP, K. (1992) *Everyone Belongs: mainstream education for children with severe learning difficulties*, London, Souvenir Press.

PAYNE, T. (1992) 'It's cold in the other room', *Support for learning*, 6(2), pp. 61–5

SAYER, J. (1987) 'Secondary schools as a resource for everyone's learning' in BOOTH, T. and POTTS, P. (eds) *Integrating Special Education*, Oxford, Blackwell/The Open University.

ACKNOWLEDGEMENTS

Grateful acknowledgement is made to the following for permission to reproduce material in this unit:

Text

Letter on page 35, reproduced courtesy of Sally Davies;

Illustrations

Figures

Figure 1: Harris, N. (1995) *The Law Relating to Schools*, Tolley Publishing Company Ltd, © Neville S. Harris 1995; *Figure 2:* DFEE (1994) *Circular 6/94, The Organisation of Special Education Provision*, © Crown copyright, reproduced with the permission of the Controller of Her Majesty's Stationery Office;

Photographs

Pages 7, 8, 12, 19, 20, 21, 22, 23 and 27: Mike Levers, The Open University.

Cartoon

Page 44: 'Touché' from *The Lady on the Bookcase* in *The Beast in Me and Other Animals* by James Thurber (Hamish Hamilton, 1949), copyright © James Thurber, 1949, reproduced by permission of Hamish Hamilton Ltd and Rosemary Thurber.

E242: UNIT TITLES

Unit 1/2   Making Connections

Unit 3/4   Learning from Experience

Unit 5   Right from the Start

Unit 6/7   Classroom Diversity

Unit 8/9   Difference and Distinction

Unit 10   Reading Critically

Unit 11/12   Happy Memories

Unit 13   Further and Higher

Unit 14/15   Power in the System

Unit 16   Learning for All